THE ATLAS OF
SPACE ADVENTURES

HOW THE APP WORKS

This atlas includes a free app* that allows you to use your smartphone or tablet to get more information from each page. Follow the steps below to download the app and launch it to discover video clips from the Universe.

*The **AtlasofSpaceAdventures** app runs on iOS (11 or later) and Android (7 or later).
iOS: *iPhone* SE, 6s, 6s Plus, 7, 7 Plus, 8, X; all *iPad Pro* models and *iPad* (2017 onwards).
Android: you can find a complete list of compatible devices by scanning the QR code on the back of the cover or by visiting https://developers.google.com/ar/discover/supported-devices#google_play

1 DOWNLOAD THE APP

The app is available free of charge from App Store and Google Play. Type in "AtlasOfSpaceAdventures" and look for the icon shown here. The information pages on each app store will tell you what operating system and device you will need to run the app. Click on the icon to download the app onto your smartphone or tablet.

2 LAUNCH AND SCAN

Launch the app. You will be asked to authorise access to your camera. The app works best in strong light and with flattened pages. Hover with your smartphone or tablet at least a foot above the pages (from 6 to 47). Large bouncy red dots will pop up on your screen.

3 WATCH, LISTEN, LEARN

Tap the red dots with your finger to trigger the videos. Sit back and enjoy the show!
This book has 50 videos.

First published in Great Britain
in 2021 by NQ Publishers,
an imprint of Nextquisite Ltd.
Copyright ©2019 by Nextquisite Ltd
Revised updated edition ©2021
by Nextquisite Ltd

www.nqpublishers.com
www.nextquisite.com

Project Director Anne McRae
Illustrations MUTI
Text Anne McRae
Editing Jane Mallet
Consultant   Dr Stephen P. Maran
Layout   Marco Nardi

ISBN: 978-1-912944-72-9

Printed in Slovakia

THE ATLAS OF
SPACE ADVENTURES

Text by Anne McRae
Illustrations by MUTI

Consultant
Dr Stephen P. Maran

NQ
PUBLISHERS
For enquiring minds

TABLE OF CONTENTS

LIFE

Although we like to think that we are not alone in the Universe, scientists have never found convincing evidence of life beyond our planet. On Earth, we have millions of different species of plants and animals, from tiny bacteria made up of just one cell, to complex creatures like whales and humans that are each composed of trillions of cells.

If we do find life elsewhere, it's very unlikely that it will look anything like this guy.

PLANET EARTH

Welcome aboard! You are in for a series of breathtaking adventures that will take you to the very origins of the Universe. But before we set out, let's take a closer look at our home planet to see what makes it so special. The Earth is unique in many ways. Firstly because it has life. Not just people, but all the plants and animals that co-exist here. Our planet also has lots of water, which is probably where life began, and an atmosphere rich in gases like oxygen, which sustain life.

DAY & NIGHT

As the Earth orbits the Sun, it also spins on itself, making one complete rotation every 24 hours*. The side facing the Sun is bathed in light and it is daytime, while the side facing away is in dark nighttime.

Sunlight

Daytime

Nighttime

*1 Earth day = 23.934 hours

SEASONS

The Earth orbits the Sun once every 365 days*. We have seasons because the Earth's axis is slightly tilted. As it goes round the Sun, the axis alway points in the same direction so during the year different parts of the Earth get more direct sunlight.

Here you can see the seasons in the Northern Hemisphere.

*1 Earth year = 365.25 days

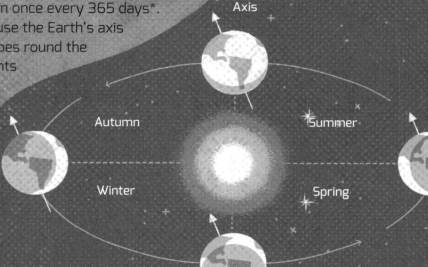

Axis

Autumn

Winter

Summer

Spring

THE EARTH BENEATH OUR FEET

We live on the Earth's thin outer layer, called the crust. If you could tunnel through it, you would find a thick sludgy layer of molten rock called the mantle. Keep going and you would run into the outer core, made of liquid iron and nickel, then the solid metallic inner core.

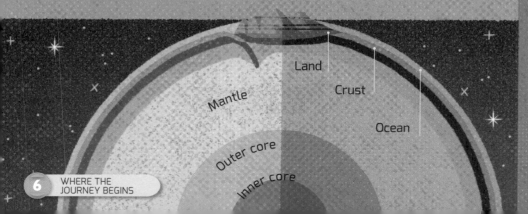

Land

Mantle

Crust

Ocean

Outer core

Inner core

Our planet is wrapped in a coat of gases called the atmosphere which is held in place by gravity. The atmosphere makes life possible on Earth. It keeps us warm while shielding us from dangerous ultraviolet sunlight. Best of all, it is full of oxygen for us to breathe.

The atmosphere has five main layers.

THE SKY ABOVE

Exosphere

Thermosphere

Mesosphere

Stratosphere

Troposphere

Earth

THE BLUE PLANET

When viewed from space, our planet looks like a blue ball. This is because more than 70 per cent of the Earth's surface is covered in water. Ours is the only planet in the Solar System that has lots of liquid water and scientists think that this is where life first evolved. We have all sorts of water on Earth, in rivers, lakes, marshes and ponds, but most of it is in the oceans. They hold 97 per cent of all the water. But why does this make the planet look blue? Because water absorbs long wavelength colours such as red, orange and yellow and it reflects short wavelength colours like blue.

SPACE JUNK

The first satellite was called Sputnik 1. It was launched into orbit around the Earth by the Soviet Union in 1957. Since then more than 8,100 others have been sent into orbit from many different countries. Of these, almost 5,000 are still going round but only about 1,900 are still working. Luckily there is plenty of space in space and they don't bump into each other!

Satellites do many different things. Some, like the Hubble Space Telescope or the ISS (see pages 8–9), help scientists to explore space. Others are for communications, military observation, weather forecasting, and navigation systems, like GPS.

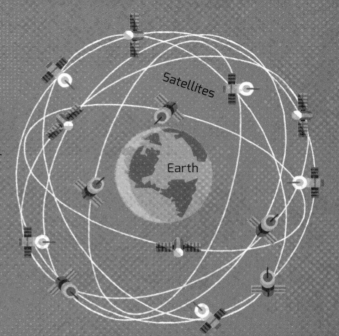

Satellites

Earth

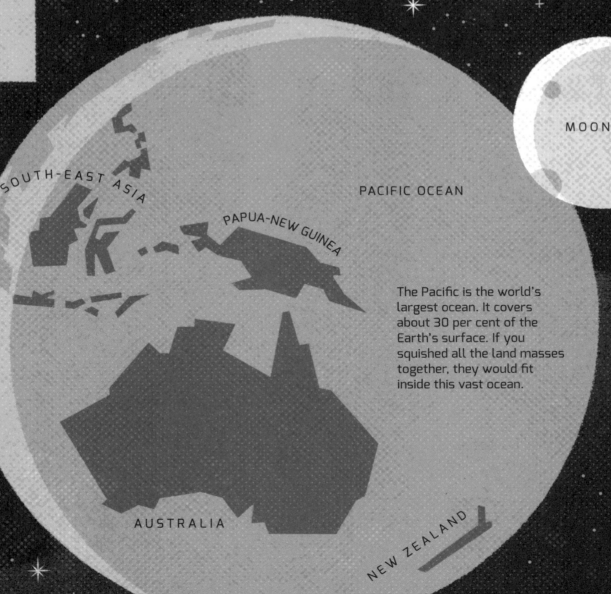

SOUTH-EAST ASIA

PAPUA-NEW GUINEA

PACIFIC OCEAN

MOON

The Pacific is the world's largest ocean. It covers about 30 per cent of the Earth's surface. If you squished all the land masses together, they would fit inside this vast ocean.

AUSTRALIA

NEW ZEALAND

SUN

LIVING IN SPACE

Our first adventure is a quick trip to the ISS (International Space Station), the longest permanently inhabited space place. To get there, we will hitch a ride on a Russian Soyuz rocket leaving from a cosmodrome in Kazakhstan. It's not far, but docking at the ISS can be tricky. It can take several hours to get perfectly aligned with the swiftly moving space station. Once on board we will join the crew for a delicious meal of freeze-dried, low moisture, pre-cooked and dehydrated space food!

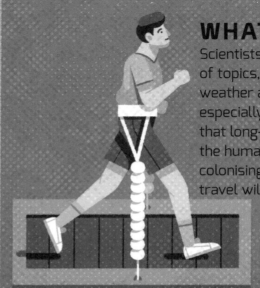

WHAT'S IT FOR?

Scientists on the ISS study a range of topics, from astronomy to the weather and medicine. They are especially interested in the effects that long-term space living has on the human body. Future plans for colonising planets and interstellar travel will depend on this.

The human body loses muscle and bone mass in zero gravity, so ISS astronauts work out for at least two hours every day. Note that our jogger is tied to the treadmill so he doesn't float away.

SPOT THE STATION: The ISS is the third brightest object in the night sky, after the Moon and Venus. To see it passing overhead, visit http://spotthestation.nasa.gov for a list of sightings.

THE ISS

The ISS is the largest spacecraft ever built. At a cost of over US$120 billion, it is also the most expensive object ever made. The ISS is in low-Earth orbit, just 400 km (250 miles) up. It whooshes along at about 27,600 km/h (17,150 mph) and completes an orbit of the Earth every 92 minutes. The ISS is always staffed by at least three crew, with room for up to seven more visitors at any one time. Crew members usually stay for about six months.

ISS crew members see 16 sunrises and sunsets every day.

Central truss

Robotic arm

Solar panels

The ISS is built upon a central truss. It has eight pairs of solar panels that make electricity from sunlight.

KITSET ISS

Sixteen countries were involved in building the ISS. About the size of a football field, it was built in space, module by module, starting in 1998.

Astronauts dangle above the Earth as they secure new modules to the ISS. Most of the building work was completed by 2011.

Supplies of food, air, water and equipment are delivered regularly by uncrewed spacecraft. Supply missions are made by the Russian Progress spacecraft, European Automated Transfer Vehicles, Japanese Kounotori vehicles, and American Dragon and Cygnus spacecraft.

There are two loos on the ISS. Urine is filtered and returned to station's drinking water supply.

The first Gateway modules will be in place in 2024. There will be space for four crew members. Because it is so far away and very expensive, the station may not be permanently inhabited. Canada, ESA and Japan will also contribute to Gateway.

Earth

Moon

Gateway

THE FUTURE

The ISS will close by 2030, if not before. China intends to have a permanently inhabited space station in orbit in the 2020s. NASA has plans for a new space station called Gateway that will orbit the Moon, where it will be perfectly positioned for activities on the Moon as well as for deep space missions.

PRIVATE SPACE

In a new departure, private companies are now venturing into space, or planning to. Commercial space stations plan to sell research space to scientists and they might even open hotels where we could take a space holiday.

The world's first private space station might look something like this one, designed by US company Axiom.

HOW THE MOON FORMED

After Earth formed, a small planet struck it, broke apart and hurled Earth rock into space. Bits of Earth and planet merged, forming the Moon.

Earth

Small planet

1. A small planet hurtles towards the Earth.

2. The impact smashes the small planet and ejects Earth rock.

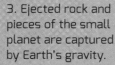

3. Ejected rock and pieces of the small planet are captured by Earth's gravity.

Earth

Moon

4. Gradually the bits shape themselves into our round Moon.

MOON BASE

A Moon base would be a safe haven in the event of a catastrophe on Earth. But it would also be the perfect launch pad for establishing a colony on Mars and exploring the rest of the Solar System and deep space. The Moon's gravity is only 17 per cent of the Earth's, so it is much easier to launch a spaceship from there.

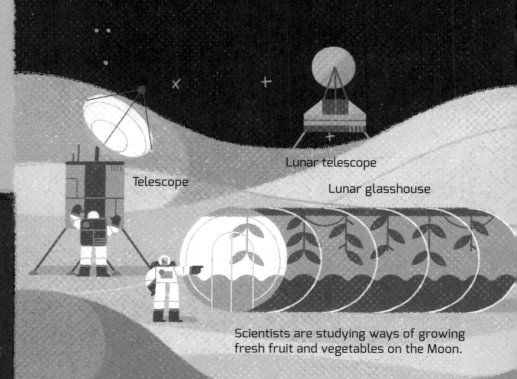

Telescope

Lunar telescope

Lunar glasshouse

Scientists are studying ways of growing fresh fruit and vegetables on the Moon.

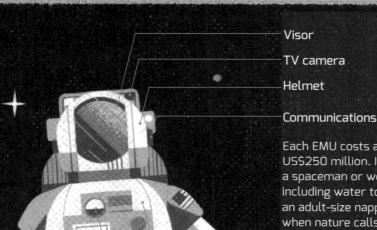

Visor

TV camera

Helmet

Communications

Each EMU costs about US$250 million. It has everything a spaceman or woman needs, including water to drink and an adult-size nappy for when nature calls.

Hard upper suit

Temperature control valve

Control module

Gloves

Lunar boots

SUITED UP

Outside a spaceship or base, people need to wear heavy-duty space suits, such as NASA's EMU (Extra-Vehicular Mobility Unit). The suit blocks out dangerous radiation and cold while providing air to breathe.

TO THE MOON

The next stop is our nearest neighbour, the Moon. At about 385,000 km (239,000 miles) from Earth, in cosmic terms the Moon is right next door. Yet people have not set foot on it since the last Apollo mission in December 1972. Space travel requires state-of-the-art technology and comes with a hefty price tag. Moonlanders need a launcher (to get off the ground), a rocket (for the three-day journey), a capsule (to carry the crew), and a landing module. Scientists from several countries, and even some private companies, are planning to return to the Moon. They intend to establish a colony there within a decade or two. As space tourism develops, you may even be lucky enough to walk on the Moon yourself!

Earth

Venus

Solar panels make electricity during lunar day; some is stored for use at night.

Moon buggy

Underground buildings protect humans from radiation and cold.

Small Base One

Lunar Inn Luxury Dome

Living on the Moon for months at a time will show how the human body adapts to living in space, without being too far from home if something goes wrong.

Sublunar Base Two

APOLLO 11

People first landed on the Moon in July 1969. US astronauts Neil Armstrong and Buzz Aldrin planted the flag, spoke to the President, then collected a few rock samples before returning to the lunar module.

Planet Earth

Buzz Aldrin salutes after ramming the US flag into the hard lunar surface.

Specially designed US Moon flag

Spacesuit

Lunar module Eagle

Apollo 11 landed on a smooth, flat area called the Sea of Tranquility.

Seismometer

TO THE SUN

Today's mission is a hot one, in every sense of the word: We're off to the Sun! Our journey will be around 150 million km (93 million miles) and since we will be travelling at the speed of light, we'll be there in about eight minutes. Although we call it the Sun, it is actually a star, just like all the other stars we can see in the night sky, but a lot closer. Like most stars, our Sun is a huge, fiery ball of gas. In its core, hydrogen is converted into helium in a process called nuclear fusion, and this generates a vast amount of energy that is emitted as heat and light. The Sun makes up 99.8 per cent of the mass of our Solar System and its immense gravity keeps all the planets, moons, asteroids and comets in orbit around it.

CONVECTION ZONE
In this area, the Sun's energy churns around.

PHOTOSPHERE
The atmospheric layer from which light shines on us.

RADIATIVE ZONE
Energy from the core works its way out to the surface. It can take 100,000 years to cross this zone.

CORE
The Sun's core is like a giant nuclear reactor. The temperature is about 15 million°C (27 million °F)!

If we could capture the energy the Sun generates in just one second, it would supply all our energy needs on Earth for 500 million years.

CORONA
The outer layer of the Sun's atmosphere.

SUNSPOTS
The dark patches on the Sun's surface are known as sunspots. They are caused by changes in the Sun's magnetic field and appear in an 11-year cycle.

SOLAR WIND

The Sun's corona gives off a stream of charged particles called the solar wind that blows out across the Solar System at almost a million miles an hour. Luckily, the Earth has a magnetic field that shields us from this wind, although very powerful solar storms can knock out power networks and satellites. Some scientists have thought of building spaceships with huge sails that capture this wind, propelling them across the Solar System without the need for fuel.

The Parker Solar Probe as it launches from Cape Canaveral. The probe will try to unlock the secrets of the solar wind and also explain why the Sun's corona is hotter than its surface, among other things.

SKIMMING THE SUN

In August 2018 NASA launched one of its hottest — and coolest — missions yet. The Parker Solar Probe is about the size of a small car and it has already broken two major space records: It has travelled faster than any other human-made object and it has gone closer to the Sun than any other spacecraft. It will break these two records again and again over the next six years, reaching a top speed of around 695,000 km/h (430,000 mph) in 2024.
At its closest approach to the Sun in 2025, the probe will swoop into the corona, or outermost atmosphere, at just 6 million km (3.8 million miles) from its surface.

PARKER SOLAR PROBE
The probe is named for Eugene Parker, the scientist who explained what causes the solar wind.

SOLAR FLARES
Massive solar flares erupt on the surface of the Sun when stored magnetic energy is suddenly released.

The Parker Space Probe is protected by a 12-cm (4.5-in) thick shield that can fly through temperatures up to almost 1400°C (2,500°F).

HOT TICKET

NASA invited people to submit their names online to be placed on a microchip aboard the probe.

More than 1.1 million names were sent and they are now on board the probe as it makes its historic journey.

FLYBYS

The Parker Probe completed its fifth successful flyby of the Sun in June 2020. It will make 19 more over the next five years.

Flybys
Sun

THE SOLAR SYSTEM

Before we continue our adventures, let's step back for a moment and take stock of the neighbourhood. We need to plan our next journeys. Earth is one of eight planets that orbit the Sun. But there are also millions of asteroids and billions of comets, as well as minor planets and moons, dust and gas, all whirling around the Sun in the shape of a vast spinning disc. This is our Solar System.

HELD IN ORBIT

The more massive an object, the more gravity it has. The Sun is so massive that its gravity pulls all the objects in the Solar System towards it. But these objects, which are moving very rapidly, try to fly away from the Sun, into outer space. The result is that everything is held in orbit, balanced between flying towards the Sun, and escaping into space.

THE PLANETS

The eight planets are divided into two groups. The inner four, including the Earth, are small and rocky, while the outer four are large and gassy. The inner planets have hard surfaces and contain a lot of metal. Among the outer planets, the two largest — Jupiter and Saturn — are made up mainly of hydrogen and helium, and are gas giants. The two planets farthest from the Sun — Uranus and Neptune — are composed of different types of ice, and are called ice giants.

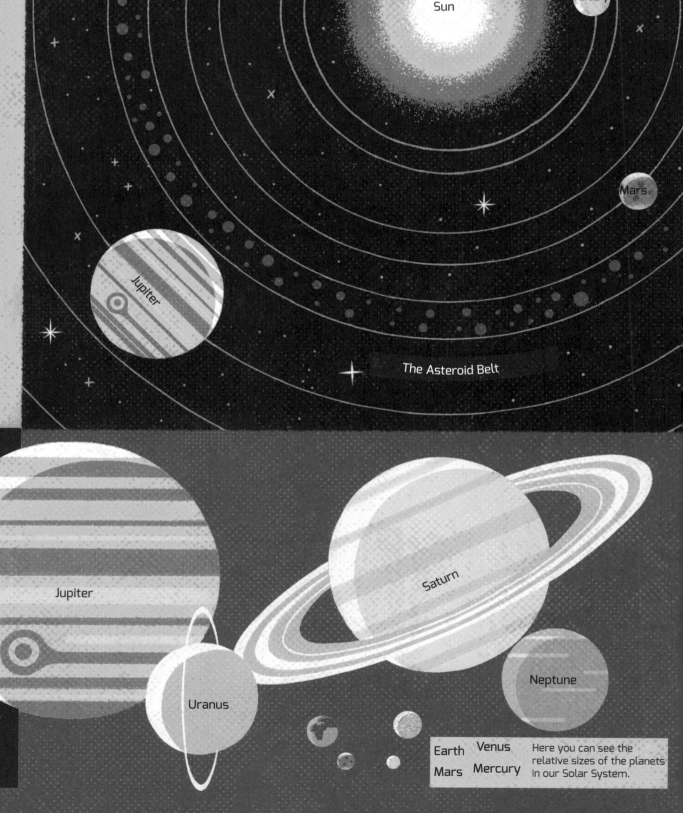

Earth
Venus

Mercury

Sun

Mars

Jupiter

The Asteroid Belt

Jupiter

Saturn

Uranus

Neptune

Earth   Venus   Here you can see the
Mars   Mercury   relative sizes of the planets
                    in our Solar System.

BIRTH OF THE SOLAR SYSTEM

Our Solar System formed about 4.6 billion years ago from a vast cloud of interstellar gas and dust. When the cloud collapsed, probably because of shockwaves from the explosion of a nearby star, the Sun was formed. The planets clumped together around it.

Saturn

Neptune

The Kuiper Belt

Uranus

1. A giant cloud made up of dust, hydrogen and other gases drifts through the Universe.

2. The cloud collapses on itself. The centre becomes so hot that nuclear fusion begins and our Sun is born. It is surrounded by a spinning disc of gas and dust.

3. The material spinning around the Sun gradually begins to clump together, and the planets and their moons are formed.

4. Today the planets in our Solar System are distinct, but there are still bits of leftover building materials, especially in the asteroid belt and much further out, in the Kuiper Belt.

DWARF PLANETS

The Solar System also has an unknown number of dwarf planets. So far, only five have been officially recognised but there are hundreds more in waiting. Dwarf planets are round-ish and they orbit the Sun on their own. With the exception of Ceres, all the dwarf planets are found on the edges of the Solar System, in the Kuiper Belt.

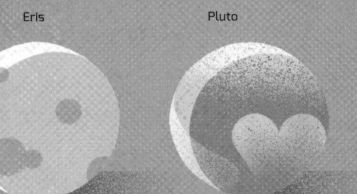

Eris

Pluto

Haumea

Makemake

Ceres

MERCURY'S MYSTERIES

Mercury is the least explored of the inner planets. Only two missions have visited: Mariner 10 (1974-5) and Messenger (20011-15). They provided a lot of information but the new BepiColombo mission still has many riddles to solve.

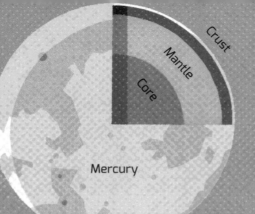
Mercury

Crust
Mantle
Core

STRUCTURE
Mercury has a very large iron core. Perhaps the Sun vaporised the planet's surface when it was forming, or it may have crashed into another object, knocking its surface away.

ORBIT
Mercury whizzes around the Sun in just 88 days, faster than any other planet. Its orbit is highly elliptical — meaning that one end of the orbit is much nearer the Sun than the opposite end. We don't know why.

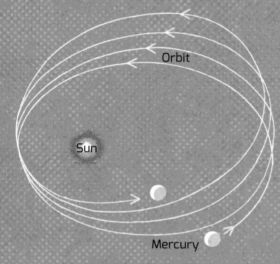
Orbit
Sun
Mercury

Ideas for colonies include burrowing underground or building large domes filled with oxygen extracted from the local rock. Mercury has ice at its poles which could be melted inside the domes to create vapour and for irrigation. Gradually, a habitable climate would form inside the domes.

BEPICOLOMBO

This exciting new mission to Mercury launched in 2018 and will enter Mercury's orbit in 2025. The joint European and Japanese spacecraft has three components that launched together but will split up when they reach Mercury. They will investigate the planet's origins, structure, craters and magnetic field, among other things.

Mercury

Thick insulation to stand high temperatures

Solar panels

MERCURY

Best to brace yourselves for this trip! We're planning to visit Mercury, the smallest planet in the Solar System and the closest to the Sun. Although Mercury is not the hottest body in the Solar System, it experiences the biggest temperature swings of any planet. Without a special spacesuit, you would roast at 430°C (800°F) during the day, while at night you would be flash-frozen as temperatures dipped below -180°C (-290°F). With little atmosphere to protect it, the planet is pelted with asteroids, as its pockmarked surface shows. On second thoughts, perhaps we will just fly by today, gazing down at the barren surface but knowing that hundreds of years from now we may have a colony there.

COULD WE COLONISE MERCURY?

Life on Mercury would be challenging. As well as the extremes of heat and cold, the planet has almost no atmosphere. Even so, people are attracted by Mercury's resources. If it could be mined, Mercury has enough minerals to meet our needs for centuries. Its closeness to the Sun means that it would be an excellent source of energy. This could be harvested with vast solar panels and beamed back to Earth or to colonies on the Moon or elsewhere in the Solar System.

A colony on wheels would be one way to beat Mercury's deadly climate. The colony would move to stay in the twilight zone between day and night where temperatures are bearable. Mercury rotates slowly and one day lasts for the equivalent of 58.6 Earth days, so the idea is not as crazy as it sounds.

A mobile colony on Mercury hundreds of years in the future.

Mercury has no natural satellites, or moons.

Mercury has one of the largest impact craters in the Solar System: the Caloris Basin. About 1,560 km (960 miles) across, it must have been hit by a body at least 100 km (60 miles) in diameter.

Asteroid

Caloris Basin

Comet

MERCURY

Asteroid

CRATERS

Messenger mapped the planet and we know that parts of Mercury's surface are densely scarred with craters formed by collisions with asteroids and comets. Other parts are smooth and there are tall cliffs and long ridges.

Messenger

NASA's Messenger added another crater when it crashed into Mercury in 2015.

VENUS

Venus is such a hostile place that it is often called Earth's hellish twin. At first glance the two planets seem alike; they are roughly the same size, have a similar composition and mass, and are about the same distance from the Sun, but that's where the similarities end. Venus is cloaked in thick clouds that prevent us from seeing its surface, although space probes have peered though them to view a barren world below. The clouds are full of sulphuric acid and the atmosphere is so heavy that pressure on the planet's surface is 90 times greater than on Earth. If you also consider that Venus is the hottest planet in the Solar System, with day temperatures soaring to 470°C (880°F), you will understand why we will not be landing there today!

VENERA-D

This Russian mission to Venus is planned for launch in 2029 or 2031. It will have an orbiter and a lander which will survive on the planet for two hours. Several Venera spacecraft have landed on Venus. In fact, in 1967, Venera 4 was the first spacecraft ever to land on another planet. These probes only lasted an hour or two but sent back a lot of vital information.

MOUNTAINS & VOLCANOES

Maat Mons is a massive volcano that stands 8 km (5 miles) tall. There are other volcanoes on Venus but this is the tallest. Venus also has mountain ranges.

VAMP

This aircraft, known as VAMP (Venus Atmospheric Manoeuverable Platform), is a concept for a mission that would explore the planet's atmosphere for signs of life and also take atmospheric measurements. Developed by private space companies, it would hitch a lift to Venus on another spacecraft, perhaps even Venera-D (see above).

VAMP aircraft

GREENHOUSE EFFECT

Most sunlight can't get through the thick clouds above Venus. What little does hit the surface turns into heat but can't escape again because of the clouds. This is what makes Venus so hot.

Some sunlight does get through

Clouds reflect most sunlight

Thick clouds

Sunlight turns into heat

Heat can't escape

FLOATING COLONIES

For a while NASA toyed with a startling idea for exploring Venus. Called HAVOC (High Altitude Venus Operational Concept), it consisted of Zeppelin-like airships filled with helium floating over the toxic clouds about 50 km (30 miles) above Venus. In the end it was decided that the HAVOC mission would be incredibly complex and it was archived.

Permanent floating airships

HAVOC airship

Some scientists think that Venus might be hiding some fabulous secrets under its clouds. Billions of years ago, when the Sun was cooler, Venus may have had primitive life. As one astrobiologist put it "If Venus didn't have life, then we really don't understand why Earth has life."

RED PLANET

Mars is covered in a layer of iron-rich red rocks and dust. High winds often whip up dust storms that can last for weeks. There is very little water on Mars and it is frozen solid. Both poles are covered in frozen water, or ice caps.

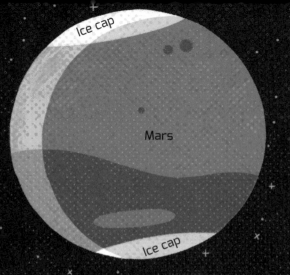

Ice cap

Mars

Ice cap

STARMAN

Dummy Starman

In 2018 Elon Musk, founder of the private space company SpaceX, shot his Tesla Roadster into orbit. It was loaded on his Falcon Heavy rocket, the most powerful existing rocket. Complete with a dummy driver, it blared David Bowie's *Life on Mars* as it slipped into orbit around the Sun.

MOONS

Phobos

Deimos

Mars has two moons called Deimos and Phobos. They are both small and oddly shaped, more like hunks of rock than smooth round moons like our own.

PERSEVERANCE

This car-sized rover touched down in the Jezero crater on Mars in 2021. Its objectives are to study the rocks and soil for signs of past life, to gather samples that will be returned to Earth by future missions, and to test technologies that will one day help humans to survive on Mars.

Perseverance has a range of high-tech cameras and sensors to record and analyse its findings on the surface of Mars.

MARS COLONY

The first Mars colony will be established by 2040, if not before. We have most of the technology already. Chinese, American and Russian governments are all researching Mars colonies, along with several private companies. One day you may even go to Mars yourself!

The first people on Mars will probably live in space domes where they will be protected from the extreme cold, low pressure, high radiation and lack of oxygen in the air. Alternatively, they may live underground,

Mars domes

Mars mobile

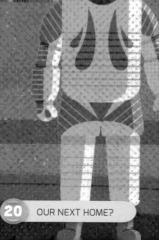

Mars spacesuits, known as "field suits," will be extra tough. Mars is extremely cold and the air is almost all carbon dioxide. Even a small hole in a suit would be deadly.

MARS

Now we are zooming over the red planet, ready to touch down. Many people think that Mars will be the first place to have a permanent space colony. But before we get to that, let's check out some Martian stats: Roughly half the size of Earth, the red planet has no liquid water and is completely covered in toxic barren rocks and sand. Mars is the fourth planet from the Sun, and much colder than Earth. It lacks the gravity to hold onto a dense atmosphere and there is almost no oxygen in its air. At 24.6 hours, a Martian day is just slightly longer than an Earth day, and the planet has seasons as we do, but they are longer and more extreme. Mars may once have harboured life but it is a very hostile place now, especially for humans. Colonising the red planet is possible, but it will be a unique and expensive challenge.

INSIGHT LANDER

NASA's InSight Lander touched down on Mars in late 2018. It soon deployed its seismometer and a heat probe to begin exploring Mars beneath the surface. It has recorded over 500 "marsquakes" and discovered a lot about the structure of the planet.

Solar panel

Solar panel

Seismometer

Heat probe

People and heavy supply loads will probably travel in separate capsules to reach the surface of Mars and land safely, as uncrewed probes already have.

Our Sun rising over Mars

Rocket

Mars farm

Spacecraft will also need to be able to leave Mars again, so that people can go home, or head off into deep space.

LUCY IN THE SKY

Launching in 2021, NASA's Lucy spacecraft will be the first to visit the Trojan asteroids. It's an exciting mission because Lucy will visit seven asteroids over 12 years. The information Lucy gathers will tell us a lot about the origins of the Solar System.

Jupiter

Trojan asteroids

LUCY

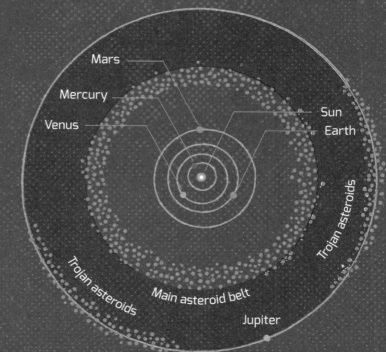

Mars

Mercury

Venus

Sun

Earth

Trojan asteroids

Trojan asteroids

Main asteroid belt

Jupiter

THE MAIN BELT & MORE

Most asteroids orbit the Sun in a belt between Mars and Jupiter. There are also two large bunches of them in the same orbit as Jupiter, known as Trojan asteroids, and thousands more scattered among the four inner planets.

COULD WE LIVE ON AN ASTEROID?

Not comfortably, and not anytime soon. Asteroids have no atmosphere, so humans would be exposed to dangerous radiation and cosmic rays. There is also weak gravity, which is hard on our bodies. We would have to build protective structures and provide artificial gravity. Mining asteroids is more probable. Many are rich in minerals such as gold and platinum. In the future, if Earth runs low on these resources, the cost of mining asteroids might pay off.

This rocket is packed with small asteroids that space miners have captured. They are being sent back to Earth to be processed.

Here's what a mining station on an asteroid might look like some time in the distant future.

ASTEROIDS

With Mars at our backs, we are racing towards the asteroid belt. We can see a few icy lumps of flying rock, or asteroids, looming ahead. They are quite far apart so there is plenty of room for us to zip through the main belt unharmed. Asteroids are bits and pieces of stuff leftover from when the Solar System was formed. The main asteroid belt is a planet that was never forged because giant Jupiter's gravity stopped the rocks from clumping together. Science fiction is full of stories about people landing on asteroids, mining their metals, and even colonising them, so let's take a closer look.

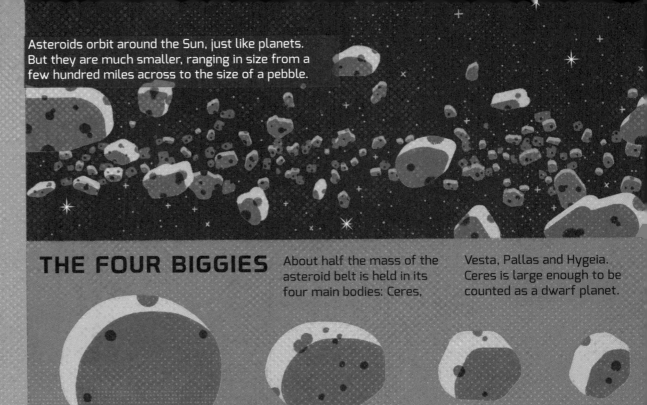

Asteroids orbit around the Sun, just like planets. But they are much smaller, ranging in size from a few hundred miles across to the size of a pebble.

THE FOUR BIGGIES

About half the mass of the asteroid belt is held in its four main bodies: Ceres, Vesta, Pallas and Hygeia. Ceres is large enough to be counted as a dwarf planet.

Ceres

Vesta

Pallas

Hygeia

DART PRACTISE

Some of the asteroids in the inner Solar System come quite close to Earth. They are known as Near Earth Objects (NEOs). Once every 10 million years or so a large asteroid hits our planet, with devastating results. Scientists keep a close eye on NEOs and they even practise what could be done to prevent a catastrophic collision. DART (Double Asteroid Redirection Test) is one such exercise.

In the unlikely event of a NEO streaking towards Earth, the best thing to do would be to try and bump it off course.

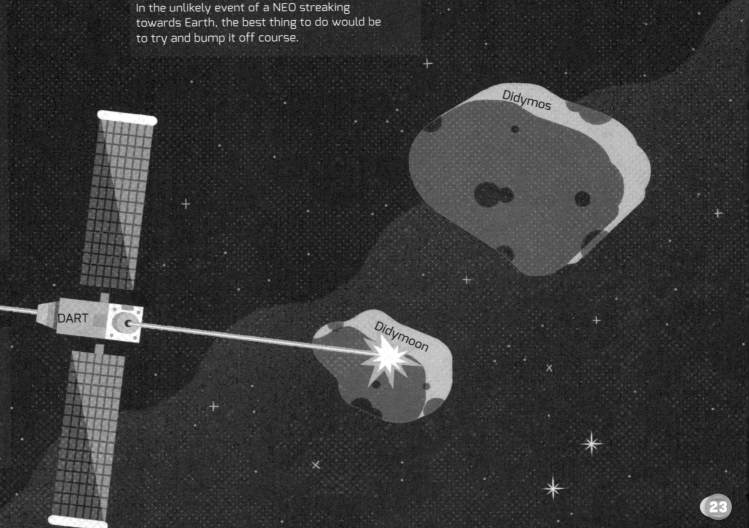

Didymos

DART

Didymoon

In 2022 NASA's DART spacecraft will approach a NEO called Didymos. This asteroid has a moonlet (nicknamed Didymoon) and this is NASA's target. DART will slam into Didymoon at about 22,000 km/h (13,500 mph) in an attempt to "nudge" it just slightly in a different direction.

JUMPING THROUGH JUPITER

You might think that if Jupiter is made of gas then you could jump right through it. There are many reasons why you can't. Firstly because you would get zapped by radiation and the gases on Jupiter would be toxic for you. Even if you wore a super-strong radiation-resistant space suit, you would be crushed by the immense pressure inside the planet and burned to a sizzle by the high temperatures.

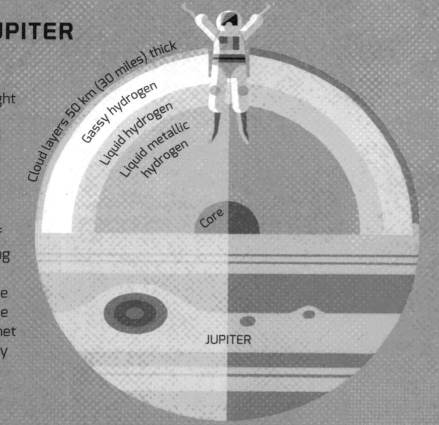

Cloud layers 50 km (30 miles) thick
Gassy hydrogen
Liquid hydrogen
Liquid metallic hydrogen
Core
JUPITER

JUPITER

Coming up now on our right is the largest planet in our Solar System: Jupiter. This gas giant has 2.5 times the mass of all the other planets combined. Jupiter is so massive that it is almost a star. If it had just a little more mass, the temperature at its core would be great enough to ignite nuclear fusion and it would shine like the Sun. Despite its great size, Jupiter spins very quickly, so much so that it bulges at the waist, and a day on Jupiter lasts less than 10 hours. We can zoom over this vast planet, admiring its striking beauty, but we can't land on it because, unlike the four inner planets, it has no solid crust. Jupiter is made almost entirely of gas.

THE GALILEAN MOONS

The Italian astronomer Galileo Galilei discovered Jupiter's four largest moons in 1610. They are all larger than the dwarf planets in our Solar System. Ganymede is the biggest moon in the Solar System and is larger even than Mercury.

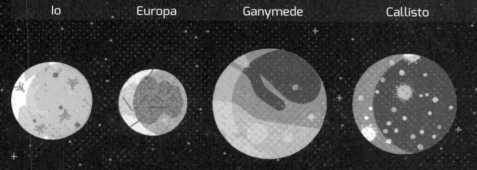

| Io | Europa | Ganymede | Callisto |

ALL THE MOONS

Jupiter has 79 moons. The moons discovered by Galilei orbit closest to Jupiter. Many of the outer moons orbit in the opposite direction to which Jupiter spins. This suggests that they are probably asteroids that were captured by the planet's gravity.

Galilean moons   Outer moons

JUICE

ESA's JUICE (Jupiter Ice Moons Explorer) will arrive at Jupiter in 2029 and start observing the planet and three of its largest moons. Among other things, it will see if it would be possible to land on Europa.

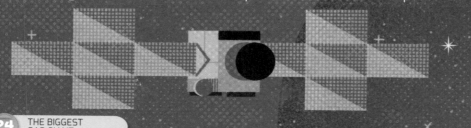

BOTTOM'S UP!

Jupiter's polar regions are not visible from Earth. Juno has sent back the first images of the poles. Scientists were amazed to find that they are covered in enormous cyclones.

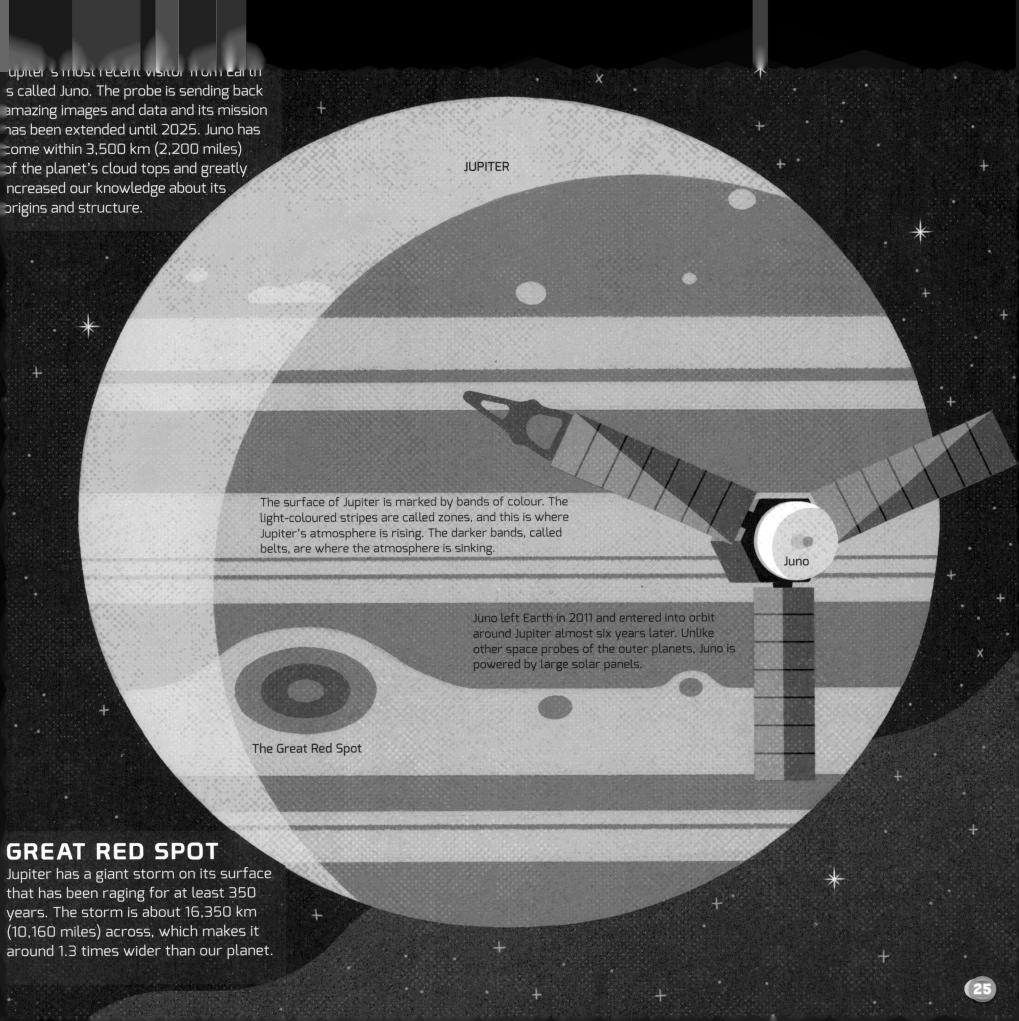

Jupiter's most recent visitor from Earth is called Juno. The probe is sending back amazing images and data and its mission has been extended until 2025. Juno has come within 3,500 km (2,200 miles) of the planet's cloud tops and greatly increased our knowledge about its origins and structure.

JUPITER

The surface of Jupiter is marked by bands of colour. The light-coloured stripes are called zones, and this is where Jupiter's atmosphere is rising. The darker bands, called belts, are where the atmosphere is sinking.

Juno

Juno left Earth in 2011 and entered into orbit around Jupiter almost six years later. Unlike other space probes of the outer planets, Juno is powered by large solar panels.

The Great Red Spot

GREAT RED SPOT
Jupiter has a giant storm on its surface that has been raging for at least 350 years. The storm is about 16,350 km (10,160 miles) across, which makes it around 1.3 times wider than our planet.

DRAGONFLY ON TITAN

NASA is planning to send a robotic probe called Dragonfly to Titan, Saturn's largest moon. Dragonfly will be like a mobile science lab and will examine the surface of Titan to look for signs of life. It will make a series of controlled take-offs and landings so that it can sample dozens of sites on different parts of the moon over two years.

Saturn

1. Dragonfly's first landing will be with the help of a parachute.

2. Dragonfly will take off and land vertically.

Titan is the second largest moon in the Solar System, after Jupiter's Ganymede. It is larger than Mercury.

3. On the ground Dragonfly will take samples of the surface and examine them, sending results back to Earth.

ODDBALL FACTS ABOUT SATURN

Saturn is huge. It's so big that nine Earths would fit side by side across its diameter, and you could squeeze 763 Earths inside it.

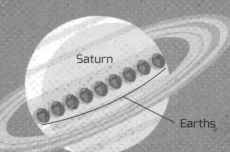

Saturn

Earths

Saturn has the second fastest winds in the Solar System. They blow at 1,800 km/h (1,118 mph) in its upper atmosphere. These gales combine with heat rising from inside the planet to make the beautiful yellow and gold stripes on its surface.

Astronaut blown away

Saturn is the least dense planet in the Solar System. It is less dense than water. If you could find a big enough ocean, it would float on top of it.

Saturn

Water

SHINY WATER WORLD

At about 500 km (310 miles) across, Saturn's sixth-largest moon, Enceladus, is not very big but it fascinates scientists. This little moon is covered in a global ocean, the top layer of which is frozen solid. Inside, Enceladus seems to make a lot of heat, but we don't know why. Some chemicals that are the building blocks of life on Earth have also been detected. All these things make scientists think that this might be a place that supports life.

Ice crust

Global ocean

Rocky core

Enceladus

Enceladus' frozen exterior reflects light, making it look shiny from afar. Jets of ice shooting from the moon feed one of Saturn's rings.

SATURN

We are now approaching Saturn, the second largest planet in the Solar System and sixth from the Sun. The view is breathtaking! Saturn is adorned with a spectacular ring system that extends 282,000 km (175,000 miles) beyond the planet itself. Despite their width, the rings are less than one km (3,300 feet) deep and each ring orbits Saturn at a different speed. In among the rings, and also well beyond them, Saturn has 82 moons. Only 13 of these are more than 50 km (30 miles) wide and just seven of them are considered major moons. Saturn itself is a gas giant, like Jupiter, and its atmosphere is made up mainly of hydrogen and helium. It is very far away and only four missions have visited: Pioneer 11, Voyagers 1 and 2 and Cassini-Huygens.

4. Examining a number of locations will give scientists a better idea of the overall conditions on Titan.

CASSINI-HUYGENS

The Cassini-Huygens mission explored Saturn for 13 years (2004–17). The spacecraft was made up of two parts, the Huygens module and the Cassini probe. They travelled together, entering Saturn's orbit in June 2004. Huygens separated from Cassini in December 2004, landed on Titan and sent data to Earth for about 90 minutes. Cassini orbited Saturn until 2017.

Cassini continued long past its original end date. In its final period it executed a number of risky manoeuvres between the planet and its rings. It was finally de-orbited and burned up in Saturn's atmosphere.

RING SYSTEM

Dutch astronomer Christiaan Huygens got the first clear view of the rings in 1655. Since then scientists have discovered that Saturn has several main ring systems, each made up of a series of narrower ringlets, so that there are actually thousands of rings circling the planet. No one knows how the rings began, but they may have been formed when icy moons or comets came too close and were torn apart by Saturn's powerful gravity.

SATURN

Saturn's rings are made up of billions of pieces of ice ranging in size from tiny specks to lumps the size of a bus.

VOYAGERS 1 AND 2

The twin NASA spacecraft Voyager 1 and Voyager 2 were launched just 16 days apart in 1977. Their original mission was to study the outer Solar System. They both explored Jupiter and Saturn then Voyager 2 went on to observe Uranus and Neptune. Both Voyagers have now crossed into interstellar space. They are still sending back scientific data via the Deep Space Network, or DSN.

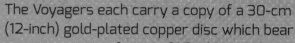

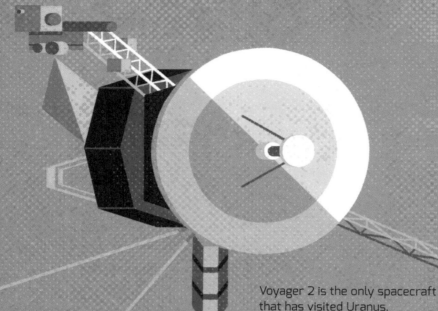

The Voyagers made some amazing discoveries, including erupting volcanoes on Jupiter's moon Io, geysers on Neptune's moon Triton and the termination shock where the solar wind slows at the very edges of our Solar System.

Voyager 2 is the only spacecraft that has visited Uranus.

THE GOLDEN RECORDS

The Voyagers each carry a copy of a 30-cm (12-inch) gold-plated copper disc which bear greetings to any forms of life they might meet. The discs have 115 images and a range of different sounds from Earth, including selections of music and spoken greetings in 55 languages.

LET'S PAY A VISIT TO TITANIA

We have touched down on Uranus's largest moon, Titania. Discovered in 1787, it measures about 1,600 km (1,000 miles) across. Titania is made of about half water-ice and half rock. It is very cold so we need our super-warm spacesuits and we are also carrying our own air supply because the moon has no atmosphere.

The view of Uranus from Titania is spectacular. We won't be staying long though. It's far too cold!

URANUS

Looming into view ahead is Uranus, the third largest planet and seventh from the Sun. Like the other gas giants, it has many moons and a ring system. But its most striking feature is that it appears to be tipped over on its side. Along with its neighbour, Neptune, Uranus is known as an "ice giant" because frozen ices of methane, water and ammonia are abundant on the planet. Uranus may also be the smelliest planet as scientists have found that its high clouds contain hydrogen sulphide, the gas that smells like rotten eggs! Uranus is far from the Sun and receives very little light or heat. It is very cold on this planet.

RINGS

The rings around Uranus are narrow and quite young. They were not formed at the same time as the planet. They are made up of dust and small pieces of dark, rocky matter. Uranus's rings were only discovered in 1977.

MOONS

Uranus has 27 known moons. They are usually divided into three groups: the 13 inner moons, the five major moons, and the nine irregular moons.

KNOCKED SIDEWAYS

Scientists think that Uranus collided with a large object just as the Solar System was forming. As it orbits the Sun, Uranus is tipped over on its side so that its equator is almost at right angles to the orbit and its poles are facing directly at or away from the Sun.

Ariel

Umbriel

URANUS

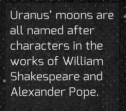
Miranda

Oberon

Uranus' moons are all named after characters in the works of William Shakespeare and Alexander Pope.

Titania

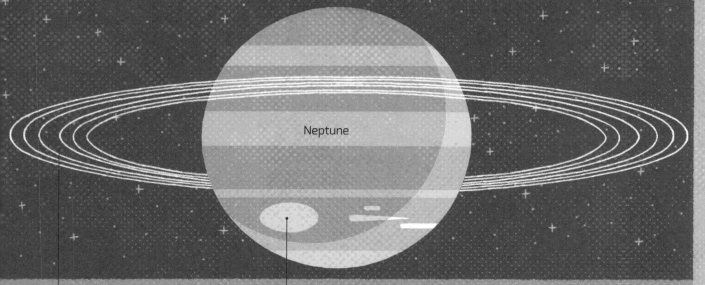

Neptune

Neptune has six faint rings, each one named for an astronomer.

In 1989 Voyager 2 spotted a giant storm similar to Jupiter's Great Red Spot. Five years later, the Hubble Telescope was unable to see it but found another storm in the planet's northern hemisphere.

NEPTUNE

As we approach Neptune, the most distant planet from the Sun, our instruments show that we are 4.3 billion km (2.7 billion miles) from home and it has taken us 12 long years to get here. If you could email the news to your friends, they would receive the message four hours after you press send. As we hover above the blue ice giant, we can see storm systems as big as the Earth in its atmosphere. With winds whipping along at about 2,400 km/h (1,500 mph), Neptune is known as the windiest planet. It gets its astonishing blue colour from the methane gas in its make up.

A CALCULATED DISCOVERY

Neptune's discovery was made in 1846 by French and British astronomers who calculated its existence using mathematics based on variations in Uranus's orbit. One year later, scientists in Berlin found the planet exactly where the astronomers had said it would be. It seems that Galileo Galilei also spotted the planet in 1613 but mistook it for a star.

Voyager 2 is the only spacecraft to have visited Neptune and we still have a lot to learn about this distant world.

STRUCTURE

Like Uranus, Neptune has an atmosphere of hydrogen, helium and methane gases. Inside, these gases are compressed into a slushy mass around a central core, probably made of rock and iron.

Gases: hydrogen, methane, helium

Upper atmosphere, clouds

Water, ammonia & methane

Rock core

Neptune

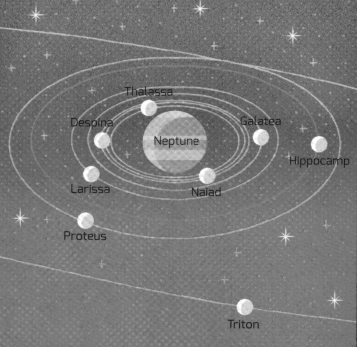

Thalassa

Despina

Galatea

Neptune

Hippocamp

Larissa

Naiad

Proteus

Triton

MOONS

Neptune has 14 known moons, all named after water gods and spirits in Greek mythology. There are seven inner moons and seven outer moons. The inner moons, shown above, have round orbits, while the outer moons loop the planet in wide ovals.

THE TRITON HOPPER

The Triton Hopper is a proposal by NASA for a lander on Triton that will use the nitrogen on the moon's surface to propel itself to a number of locations. The Hopper would take photographs and samples of the ices to analyse. It might even fly through some geysers to see what they are made of.

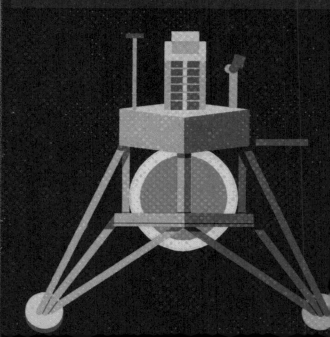

AMAZING TRITON

Triton is the biggest of Neptune's 14 moons. It was discovered in 1846 just 17 days after the planet itself. Triton is an unusual moon because it orbits its parent in the opposite direction to almost every other satellite in the Solar System. This makes scientists think that Triton is an object from the Kuiper Belt that was captured by Neptune's gravity. In about three billion years it will smash into Neptune and be utterly destroyed.

If we touch down on Triton, put on your spacesuit. With average surface temperatures of -235°C (-391°F), Triton is the coldest known body in the Solar System. There is very little atmosphere so you would need to bring your own air supply and walking in just eight per cent gravity might be hard. However, you would enjoy spectacular views of coloured ices, flat plains and gorgeous geysers.

NEPTUNE

Geyser

Geyser

Here we are on Triton looking up at Neptune as it rises over the horizon.

Voyager 2 is the only spacecraft that has ever visited Triton. It flew by in 1989 and sent back images showing the geysers of dust and nitrogen gas that erupt out of the moon's crust. They shoot icy plumes 8 km (5 miles) into the air for years on end.

31

NEW HORIZONS

The space probe New Horizons was launched in 2006 with the aim of exploring Pluto and other Kuiper Belt objects as well as the origins of our Solar System. Travelling 100 times faster than a jetliner, it reached Pluto in July 2015 and gave us our first real look at this fascinating world. From Pluto, New Horizons moved on towards a frozen KBO called Arrokoth. It completed a flyby on New Year's Day, 2019 and took over 15 months to beam all the information back to Earth. New Horizons has enough propellent to journey on for at least 20 years and astronomers are expecting more amazing information and images in the years to come.

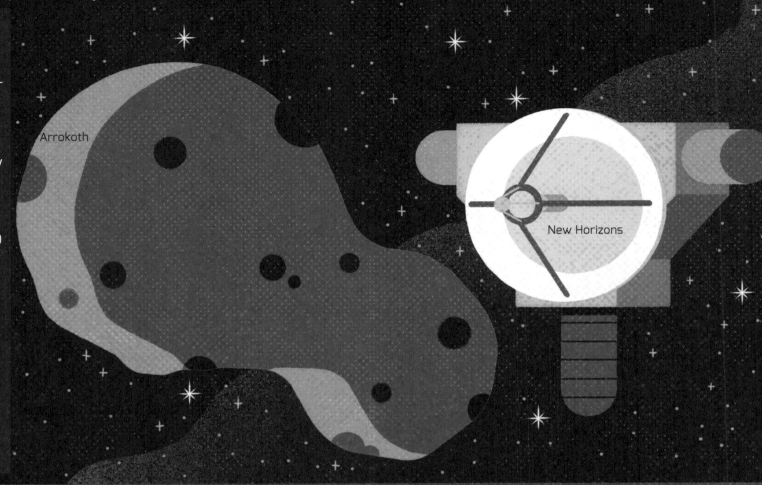

Arrokoth

New Horizons

COMETS

Comets are small icy bodies that orbit the Sun. When their orbits bring them close to the Sun they warm up and begin releasing gas and dust. This produces a brilliant, glowing head larger than most planets and a tail that can be millions of miles long. Only a few thousand comets are known and named but there are thought to be billions more in the Kuiper Belt and the Oort Cloud.

Comets are made of bits leftover from the formation of the Solar System. They are mainly ice and rock. Astronomers call them "dirty snowballs." Each comet has a small, frozen centre, called a nucleus. Comets get brighter as they approach the Sun, shedding gas and dust, then grow dimmer as they move away. Each orbit leaves them slightly smaller than the previous one.

Most comets follow long elliptical (oval) paths that take them close to the Sun for part of their orbit and then out into the farthest reaches of the Solar System for the rest.

Right: Comet orbiting the Sun

Sun

EDGES OF THE SOLAR SYSTEM

We have left Neptune far behind us and we are now venturing out to the edges of the Solar System. Looking back, the Sun is little more than a particularly brilliant star, and very little of its heat and light can be seen or felt. Soon we will enter the Kuiper Belt, with its trillions of icy bodies and dwarf planets such as Pluto and Eris. The distances are huge, and if we really could undertake this journey, it would take us more than 300 years to go from Neptune to the beginnings of the Oort Cloud. Flying across the Oort Cloud would take another 30,000 years.

You can track the journeys of Voyager 1 and 2 online. Download the app NASA's Eyes. https://voyager.jpl.nasa.gov/mission/status/#where_are_they_now

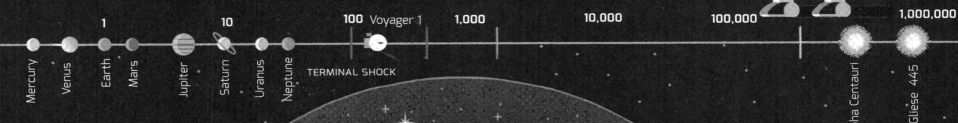

| 1 | 10 | 100 | Voyager 1 | 1,000 | 10,000 | 100,000 | 1,000,000 |

Sun | Mercury | Venus | Earth | Mars | Jupiter | Saturn | Uranus | Neptune | TERMINAL SHOCK | Alpha Centauri | Gliese 445

The diagram above shows the distance between the Sun and our nearest neighbouring star system, Alpha Centauri and another star, known as Gliese 445, which is 1,000,000 AUs from our Sun. The distances are shown in AUs (astronomical units). An AU is about 150 million km (93 million miles), or the average distance from Earth to the Sun.

Oort Cloud sphere

Sun

Oort Cloud disc

THE OORT CLOUD

Far beyond the Kuiper Belt, astronomers believe there is a huge disc surrounded by a sphere both filled with icy objects. This is known as the Oort Cloud. The Oort Cloud is so far away that it is only loosely bound to the Solar System. The edges of the Oort Cloud are considered to be the edges of the Solar System.

THE KUIPER BELT

The Kuiper Belt is a vast disc with a hole in the centre orbiting around the Sun. It extends into space from Neptune's orbit for 7.4 billion km (4.5 billion miles). This chilly expanse may hold trillions of icy bodies leftover from when the Solar System was formed. It's a lot like the asteroid belt, only here the objects (known as Kuiper Belt Objects, or KBOs) are made of ice rather than rock.

Five NASA spacecraft have reached the Kuiper Belt and three of them are still beaming back scientific information. Pioneer 10 and 11 launched in 1972 and 1973, respectively. NASA has lost contact with both. Voyager 1 and 2 have crossed into interstellar space and are still active, as is the exciting New Horizons mission.

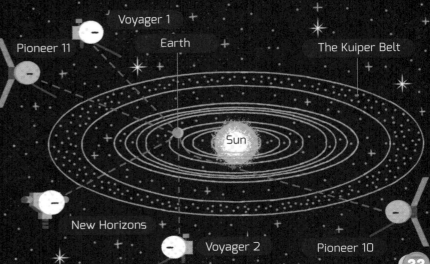

Voyager 1

Pioneer 11

Earth

The Kuiper Belt

Sun

New Horizons

Voyager 2

Pioneer 10

33

INTO THE MILKY WAY

We are safe inside our imaginary spaceship and zooming through the stars of our home galaxy, the Milky Way. From Earth we can see about 3,000 stars, but there are at least 200 billion of them in the Milky Way. If you calculate that most of the stars have planets, and many of the planets have moons, and that the galaxy also contains a lot of comets, asteroids, dust and gas, then you understand that it's quite a busy place, even if it is spread out over a vast area. If our spaceship could ride on a beam of light, it would take us 200,000 years to travel across the galaxy.

STRUCTURE

The Milky Way is a barred spiral galaxy. It has a central bar dense with stars and then four arms of stars spiralling outwards. We are about 28,000 light years from the galactic centre. Our galaxy is about 200,000 light years from one side to the other. It is quite a big galaxy, but by no means the largest. All the stars, gas and dust rotate around the black hole at the centre of the galaxy.

THE LOCAL GROUP

Galaxies tend to stay together in groups and clusters. The Milky Way is part of a group of about 50 galaxies known as the Local Group. These are our closest neighbours. In its turn, the Local Group is part of a large cluster of galaxies called the Virgo Supercluster.

VIRGO SUPERCLUSTER

Andromeda galaxy

Triangulum galaxy

THE LOCAL GROUP

Milky Way galaxy

SPACE TRAVEL

Space travel has many effects on the body, mostly bad. Astronauts have suffered from changes to their muscles, bones, hearts and blood cells. They have had trouble sleeping and suffered from flatulence (farting). There was just one plus; they grew 2 cm (1 inch) taller!

Here we are, heading out into deep space.

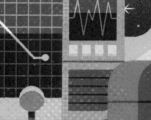
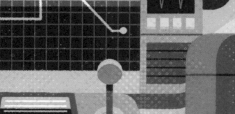

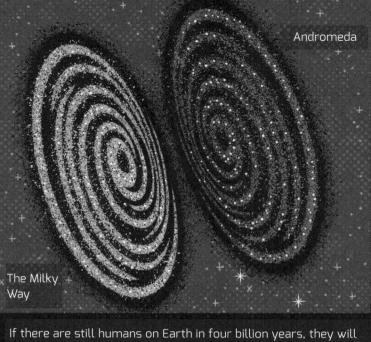
Andromeda

The Milky Way

COLLISION COURSE

The spiral galaxy closest to the Milky Way is called Andromeda. It is hurtling towards us at over 400,000 km/h (250,000 mph) and in about 4 billion years the two galaxies will collide, ripping each other apart. Gradually the black holes at the centre of each galaxy will merge and a single large galaxy will be formed.

If there are still humans on Earth in four billion years, they will have a grandstand view of the galaxies colliding. Astonishingly, astronomers think that our Solar System will probably survive the collision. The stars in each galaxy are so far apart that they won't actually run into each other.

SAGITTARIUS A*

SAGITTARIUS A*

You have probably heard about black holes, but you may not have realised that we have a monster-size black hole at the centre of our galaxy. In fact, scientists think that almost all galaxies have a supermassive black hole at their centre. Ours is called Sagittarius A* (pronounced Sagittarius A-star) and it has more than four million times the mass of the Sun. Scientists can't see Sagittarius A* because black holes are very difficult to see, but they know that it is there — at about 28,000 light years from Earth — because of the way it affects nearby objects.

A black hole is really just a lot of mass in a very small area, which things orbit around. The black hole at the centre of our galaxy is not gobbling up stars and it will not consume our galaxy. At least, not yet. At the moment it acts like an anchor and the stars in our galaxy orbit around it. Clearly, if a nearby star gets knocked off course and comes too close to the black hole, it's goners!

Exoplanets are often spotted when they cross in front of, or transit, their star. This makes it easier for telescopes on Earth or in space to see them.

Above: An exoplanet transits its star.

FINDING EXOPLANETS

Cosmologists had long suspected that at least some stars might have planets, but they were unable to find them until the 1990s when new technology made it possible to detect them.

Below: TRAPPIST-South is a robot telescope in Chile. TRAPPIST stands for "Transiting Planets and Planetesimals Small Telescope".

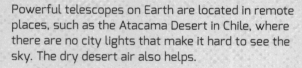

Powerful telescopes on Earth are located in remote places, such as the Atacama Desert in Chile, where there are no city lights that make it hard to see the sky. The dry desert air also helps.

Telescopes in space are even better for spying on the Universe as they are beyond the Earth's atmosphere and have a much clearer view.

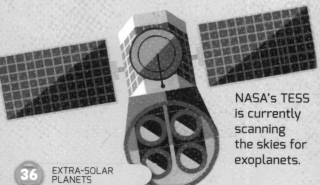

NASA's TESS is currently scanning the skies for exoplanets.

DOES ANYONE LIVE THERE?

There are different types of exoplanet. Many are small and icy while others are ice or gas giants unsuited to life as we know it. Some gas giants, known as "Hot Jupiters," orbit very close to their stars which makes them extremely hot. Some rocky planets about the same size as Earth have been found orbiting a star within the "Goldilocks zone" (an area where conditions might support life). But no proof of life has been found on any exoplanet as yet.

Rogue planet

EXOPLANETS

Now we are far beyond the edges of the Solar System and about to touch down on a planet a bit like Earth. It's called an exoplanet, or extrasolar planet, meaning that it orbits a star like our Sun but in another solar system. The closest exoplanet is Proxima Centauri b, which orbits Proxima Centauri, the nearest star to Earth. It's really exciting so you might want to use your interstellar mobile phone to call home. Mobile phones transform your voice into a signal that travels at the speed of light but if you called from here, it would take four years and two months before a phone rang on Earth!

Above: Scientists now believe that most stars have at least one exoplanet.

ROGUE PLANETS

Some planets, known as "rogue" or "interstellar planets" don't orbit a star at all. They orbit around the centre of the galaxy on their own, unbound by any star. These planets may have been thrown out of the planetary system in which they were formed, or they may never have been bound by the gravity of any star.

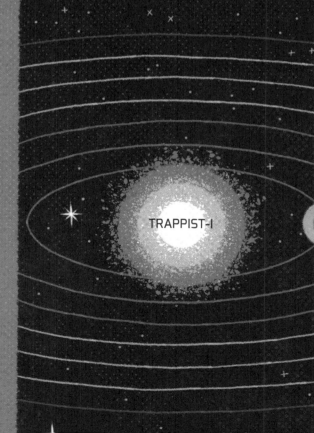

TRAPPIST-1

CAN WE VISIT?

With our current technology it would take three million years just to reach the nearest star system, so you probably won't be taking a holiday on an exoplanet anytime soon! But some scientists believe that within about 200 years we should be able to drive spaceships with a powerful beam of light, making interstellar journeys possible.

A space ticket

TRAPPIST-1

TRAPPIST-1 is a red dwarf star in the constellation of Aquarius. It was discovered in 1999 but it wasn't until 2017 that European scientists announced that they had discovered seven Earth-size rocky planets in orbit around it, more than in any other planetary system. What's more, three of the planets may have the right conditions for life.

This illustration shows all seven planets that orbit TRAPPIST-1. They are very close in and would fit within the orbit of Mercury in our own Solar System.

The three light blue planets in this diagram lie in the "Goldilocks zone" where life may exist. Conditions on the orange planets would be too hot and the most distant blue planet would be too cold.

A young space traveller of the future gazes out on the amazing landscape of an exoplanet in the TRAPPIST-1 Solar System.

STELLAR NURSERIES

Stars form inside vast, dense clouds of dust and gas, called stellar nurseries, or star-forming regions. The clouds are nudged into star formation when events stir things up. The explosion of a supernova, for example, might send shockwaves through a cloud, knocking dust and gas into clumps. Their gravity attracts more gas and dust and they grow larger and larger until the heat in their core ignites and nuclear fusion begins. Depending on the type of star, the process can take from several thousand to many millions of years.

The Mystic Mountain is beyond amazing. It is three light years (or about 28 trillion km / 18 trillion miles) tall and covered in turbulent gas streamers. Nestled inside are newborn stars.

Mystic Mountain

Here we are, still going strong! We are speeding towards the Mystic Mountain in the Carina Nebula.

LIFE CYCLE OF A STAR

A star's life begins when nuclear fusion gets underway in its core. If the star is an average star, like the Sun, then it burns steadily as a main sequence star for billions of years. When it has burned up all its hydrogen, it expands into a red giant. Gradually the red giant loses its outer layers and develops a planetary nebula around its hot core. When the nebula blows away the star becomes a white dwarf which cools and fades away. Stars with a lot more mass, known as massive stars, have relatively short lives. They burn through their gas in just a few million years before turning into supergiants, or even hypergiants, then exploding as supernovas. They leave behind either a neutron star or a black hole.

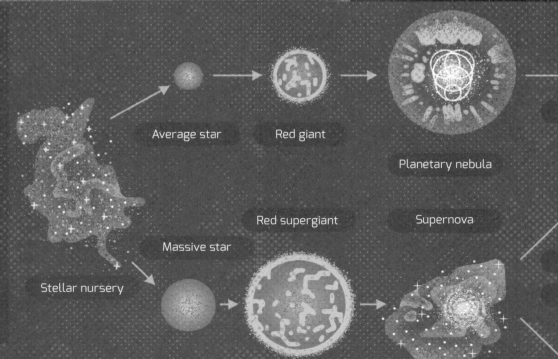

Average star

Red giant

White dwarf

Planetary nebula

Red supergiant

Supernova

Massive star

Stellar nursery

Neutron star

Black hole

STARS

Now we are flying towards the Mystic Mountain, a spectacular pillar of dust and gas in the Carina Nebula where stars are born. This is just one of many star-forming regions in our galaxy. But what exactly is a star? Like our Sun, a star is a giant, fiery ball of gas. In its core, hydrogen is converted into helium in a process called nuclear fusion. This creates energy that is radiated into space. Most stars have planets orbiting around them, like our Solar System. There are different kinds of stars: some are bigger and brighter than others, and a few end their lives in spectacular explosions before turning into black holes.

BINARY STARS

Our Sun is unusual in being a lone star. Most stars exist in groups of two or more. About three-quarters are thought to be binary, or two-star systems. Astronomers think that billions of years ago the Sun may also have had a twin, but with a very distant orbit. After about a million years together, it drifted away, mingling into the other stars in the Milky Way.

Binary stars

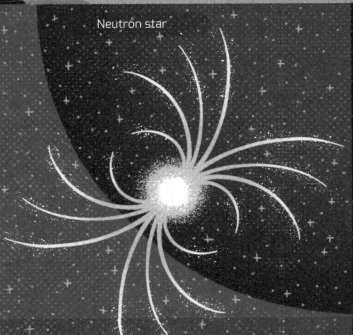

If you lived on a planet in a binary star system every day you would see double sunsets, as the two stars dipped below the horizon.

RED DWARF STARS

These stars are smaller and cooler than stars like our Sun. They burn their hydrogen slowly and live very long lives. Red dwarfs are by far the most common stars in the Milky Way. The closest star to the Sun, called Proxima Centauri, is a red dwarf.

Red dwarf star

Neutron star

NEUTRON STARS

Neutron stars form from supernovas. They are the densest objects in the Universe. As a massive star's core collapses, it spins faster and faster; newly formed neutron stars rotate at up to 600 times per second. Astronomers think that there are about 100 million neutron stars in the Milky Way.

SUPERNOVAS

When a really large star, with at least eight times the mass of the Sun, starts running out of fuel, it swells up into a supergiant. When all the fuel is gone, the star collapses and the outer layers are blasted off in a huge explosion. The energy of a supernova can be as much as all the energy released by a star like the Sun over its lifetime.

TYPES OF GALAXIES

There are four main types of galaxies: spiral galaxies, barred spiral galaxies, elliptical galaxies and irregular galaxies. Each type has more than one variation. There are also some peculiar galaxies, for example in the shape of a ring or the letter "S."

CLUSTERS & SUPERCLUSTERS

Most galaxies stay together in groups of about 50 or so, while others form massive clusters. The largest groups of galaxies are called superclusters and they have hundreds or even thousands of galaxies, each one containing billions of stars. Usually there is a giant elliptical galaxy at the centre of the cluster. Most galaxies in clusters are ellipticals, while most galaxies outside of clusters are spirals.

ELLIPTICAL GALAXIES

These galaxies are usually oval, like an egg. They often have older stars and not a lot of gas, so not many new stars are being formed. Some of the largest galaxies in the Universe are elliptical.

IRREGULAR GALAXIES

These galaxies have no particular form, sometimes because they have been pulled out of shape by the gravity of neighbouring galaxies.

SPIRAL GALAXIES

These galaxies are shaped like pinwheels. They have a central hub of stars, surrounded by at least two spiral arms with more stars.

BARRED SPIRAL GALAXIES

These are a variation on spiral galaxies. They have a bar of stars running across the centre and spiral arms leading off from there.

FROM THE SIDE

If you look at a spiral galaxy from the side (below), you will see that it has a bulge in the centre and then spreads out in the shape of a flat disc.

QUASAR

Quasars are the brightest objects in the Universe. They are supermassive black holes with matter such as gas and stars flowing into them. When a lot of matter falls into a quasar an enormous amount of energy is released and they shine very brightly.

SEYFERT GALAXY

Seyfert galaxies have much brighter centres than other galaxies.

RADIO GALAXY

Radio galaxies emit very strong radio waves.

ACTIVE GALAXIES

Active galaxies have small dense cores that blast out enormous amounts of light and other sources of energy. They produce much more energy than the stars they contain emit. Astronomers think that they have supermassive black holes at their centres. Many active galaxies also eject narrow beams of energetic particles at nearly the speed of light. Active galaxies include Seyfert galaxies, Radio galaxies, and Quasars.

GALAXIES

We have finally reached the edges of the Milky Way. Now we can see different types of galaxies. Let's look a little closer. A galaxy is a vast collection of stars, as well as gas, dust, nebulas, asteroids, comets, planets and dark matter all held together by gravity. Scientists estimate that there are at least 200 billion galaxies in the Universe, but there may be many more. Galaxies range in size from small ones, known as dwarfs, with just a few 100 million stars, to giants with over 100 trillion. The stars and other matter orbit around the galaxy's centre of gravity, which is usually a large black hole.

STARBURST GALAXIES

Starburst galaxies produce new stars at a very high rate. They contain a lot of gas and use it up quickly creating a lot of large stars. A starburst galaxy is not a separate type of galaxy but rather a phase in the lives of some galaxies. Scientists are not sure what causes them, but a collision with another galaxy may be a trigger.

A new space telescope, called the James Webb Space Telescope is scheduled to launch in 2021. It will work alongside HST and eventually replace it.

SPACE TELESCOPES

Telescopes that operate in space are much more expensive than earthbound ones but they get a far better view. The most famous space-based telescope is the Hubble (HST). It launched in 1990 and has hugely increased what we know about the Universe.

THE BIG BANG

Let's imagine that our trusty spaceship is also a time machine and can ride the light back to the origins of our Universe. What would we see at the first moment in time? Of course, no one knows for sure, but the best theory is called the Big Bang. According to this idea, the Universe sprang into being about 13.8 billion years ago. It expanded very quickly, as atoms were formed followed by stars and galaxies. Our Solar System appeared about 4.6 billion years ago. Today the Universe is still expanding and it is getter bigger at an ever increasing rate. If we could look about 22 billion years into the future, we might even see the Big Rip, when everything is torn apart and the Universe ends.

THE MULTIVERSE

Some scientists believe that there may be more than one universe. They think that our Universe is just one of many in a mind-bogglingly vast structure called a Multiverse. According to this theory, if there is one universe that came into being in a Big Bang, why should there not be more? There might be a huge and increasing number of universes, each one governed by different laws of physics. It's an amazing idea but not everyone accepts that it might be true.

DARK STUFF

The Universe is made of matter and energy. Ordinary matter, which includes all the visible things, like planets, stars and galaxies, makes up about five per cent of the Universe. A much larger part, about 25 per cent, is made up of dark matter. Scientists don't know what this dark stuff is but they can tell it exists because of the way visible matter behaves in space. The remaining 70 per cent of the Universe is made of something equally mysterious, called dark energy. Scientists don't know what dark energy is either.

The red parts in this false colour map show the dark matter between galaxies.

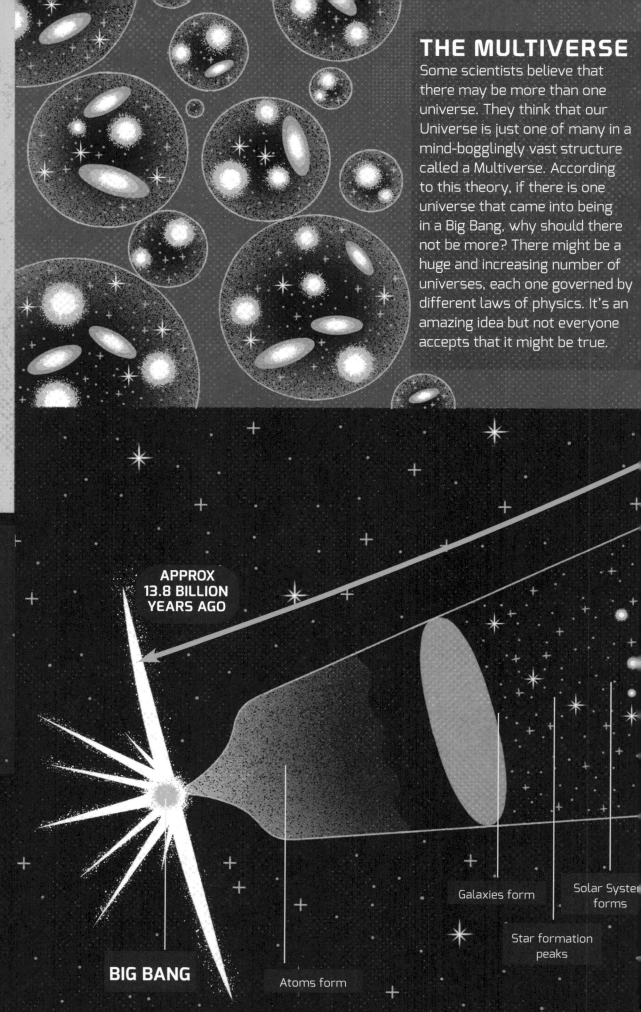

APPROX 13.8 BILLION YEARS AGO

BIG BANG

Atoms form

Star formation peaks

Galaxies form

Solar System forms

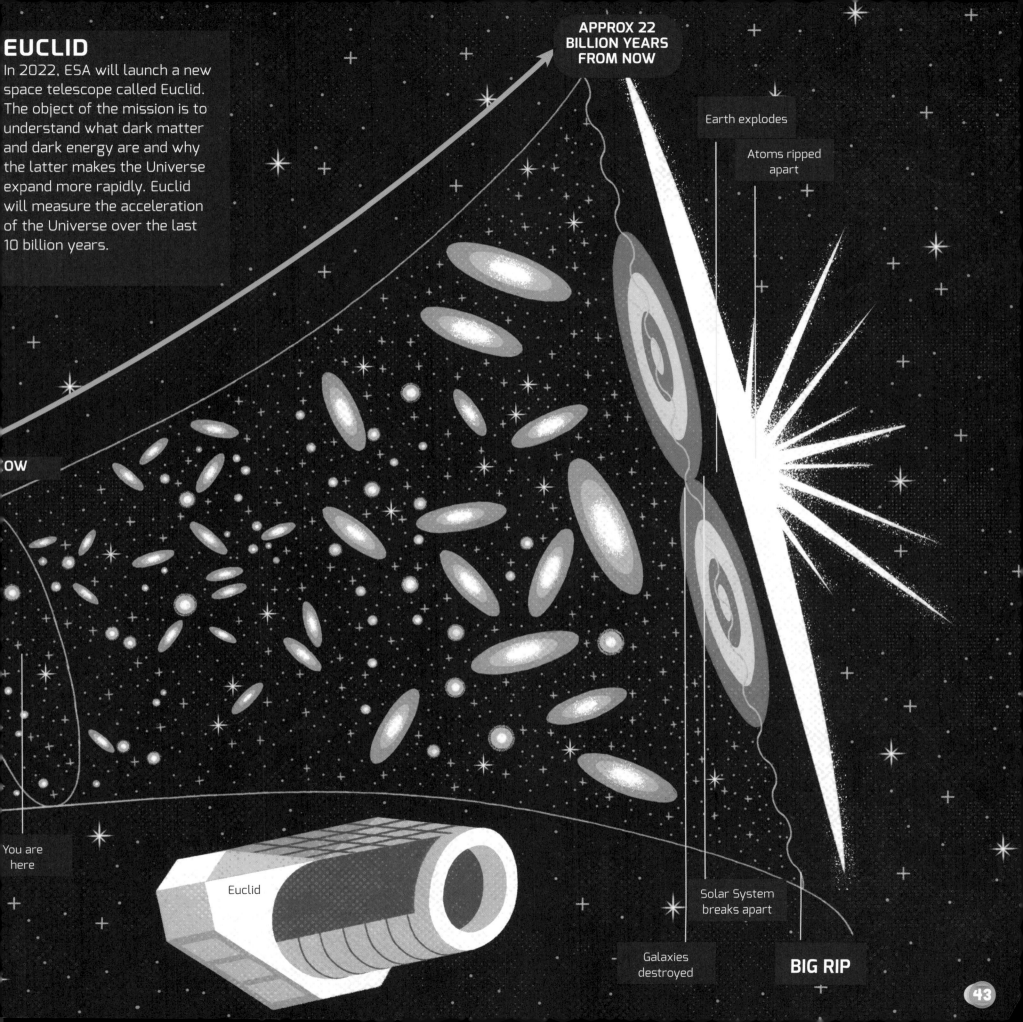

EUCLID

In 2022, ESA will launch a new space telescope called Euclid. The object of the mission is to understand what dark matter and dark energy are and why the latter makes the Universe expand more rapidly. Euclid will measure the acceleration of the Universe over the last 10 billion years.

APPROX 22 BILLION YEARS FROM NOW

Earth explodes

Atoms ripped apart

OW

You are here

Euclid

Solar System breaks apart

Galaxies destroyed

BIG RIP

LISA

In the 2030s, ESA will launch three spacecraft together that will orbit the Sun in a triangular formation several million miles apart. They will investigate gravitational waves, learning about the formation and structure of galaxies, the evolution of stars, the early Universe, and the structure and nature of time itself.

LISA Spacecraft 2

Laser beams

LISA Spacecra

LISA Spacecraft 1

A spaceship of the future hurtles towards a wormhole

WARP SPEED & WORMHOLES

The main problem in exploring the Universe is distance. One of the nearest galaxies to the Milky Way, Sagittarius Dwarf Elliptical Galaxy, is 70,000 light years away. With our current technology, that's just too far. Even if we could travel at the speed of light, which we can't, it's still too far. But, if we could travel faster than light, at what sci-fi calls "warp speed", then deep space travel would be possible. Einstein said that nothing can go faster than light, but some scientists disagree.

Wormholes are popular in science fiction. They are like holes or bridges in spacetime that would allow us to take shortcuts on long journeys across the Universe. No one has ever found a wormhole and scientists are not sure that we would survive a journey through one.

Wormhole shortcut

The long way around

WHAT DOES THE FUTURE HOLD?

That was quite a trip, wasn't it? Right to the end of the Universe! Of course, you know that most of the adventures we had in this book could not happen. Not yet, anyway. We just don't have the technology and there are so many things we still don't know. But that's what makes space so exciting. There is still so much to learn and such astonishing things to discover. In the coming decades, people will almost certainly return to the Moon and perhaps build a colony there. They may even land on Mars and colonise that planet. Space tourism may well become a popular way to spend vacation time. If resources like gold and platinum get scarce on Earth, we really might start mining asteroids. We may even discover a way to travel faster than light, so that we could travel effortlessly in deep space. Space really is the new frontier.

Wormhole

WHERE IS EVERYBODY? - SETI

SETI (aka the Search for Extraterrestrial Intelligence), is a scientific term for all the ways in which we are looking for signs of intelligent life beyond our planet. Many radio telescopes in various parts of the world constantly scan the skies searching for artificial radio signals. All their findings are analysed by supercomputers. Other projects search for laser beams of light that intelligent beings might use to communicate. They also look for alien spacecraft and probes. Scientists have even launched our own signals into space, to let other intelligent life know that we exist. We don't know if anyone has seen these messages and some scientists have even asked if it is wise to broadcast our existence to aliens who might not be peaceful or nice.

In the 1950s an Italian physicist, Enrico Fermi, said that the size and age of the Universe suggests that other intelligent life must exist. So why haven't we found any signs of it?

Lend your computer power to research! Do you want to help discover life beyond Earth? Google SETI@home

X°°#BB@**GG%!
Translates as "SEE YOU SOON!"

INDEX